The Wisdom
of the Great Chiefs

The Wisdom of the Great Chiefs

The Classic Speeches of Chief Red Jacket, Chief Joseph, and Chief Seattle

Selected and with
Chapter Introductions by
KENT NERBURN

THE CLASSIC WISDOM COLLECTION
NEW WORLD LIBRARY
SAN RAFAEL, CALIFORNIA

©1994 Kent Nerburn

The Classic Wisdom Collection
Published by New World Library
58 Paul Drive, San Rafael, CA 94903

Cover design: Greg Wittrock
Cover photo of Chief Joseph: Courtesy of Bettman Archives
Text design: Nancy Benedict
Typography: TBH Typecast, Inc.

Library of Congress Cataloging-in-Publication Data

Wisdom of the great chiefs : the classic speeches of Red Jacket,
    Chief Joseph, and Chief Seattle / collected and with
    introductions by Kent Nerburn.
        p. cm. — (The Classic wisdom collection)
    ISBN 1-880032-40-6 : $12.95
    1. Speeches, addresses, etc., Indian. 2. Red Jacket
(Seneca chief), ca. 1756–1830. 3. Joseph, Nez Perce Chief,
1840–1904. 4. Seattle, Chief, 1790–1866. I. Red Jacket
(Seneca chief), ca. 1756–1830. II. Joseph, Nez Perce Chief,
1840–1904. III. Seattle, Chief, 1790–1866. IV. Nerburn,
Kent, 1946–   . V. Series.
E98.O7W57   1994
973'.0497 — dc20   93-47415
                                                        CIP

ISBN 1-880032-40-6
Printed in the U.S.A. on acid-free paper
Distributed by Publishers Group West

10 9 8 7 6 5 4 3 2 1

The spirit of the Native people, the first people, has never died. It lives in the rocks and the forests, the rivers and the mountains. It murmurs in the brooks and whispers in the trees. The hearts of these people were formed of the earth that we now walk, and their voice can never be silenced.

— Kent Nerburn

Contents

Publisher's Preface

Life is an endless cycle of change. We and our world will never remain the same.

Every generation has difficulty relating to the previous generation; even the language changes. The child speaks a different language than the parent does.

It seems almost miraculous, then, that certain voices, certain books, are able to speak not only to one, but to many generations beyond them. The plays and poems of William Shakespeare are still relevant today — still entertaining, disturbing, and profound. Shakespeare is the writer who, in the English language, defines the word *classic*.

There are a great many other writers and thinkers who, for a great many reasons, can be considered classic, for they withstand the test of time. We want to present the best of them to you in the New World Library Classic Wisdom Collection. Even though these writers and thinkers lived many years ago, they are still relevant and important in today's world for the enduring words of wisdom they created, words that should forever be kept in print.

The Wisdom of the Great Chiefs is a very special book in this collection. It is profound, touching, and inspired. Every citizen of the planet Earth can gain value from the words and insights of these great Native American leaders.

We pray that their traditions will be remembered and will grow and prosper. We hope that this book will, in its own way, contribute to increased awareness of and respect for the wisdom of the Native American people.

Marc Allen
New World Library

Prologue

Most of us are trained to read with our minds. We pass over words, compressing them into ideas, and we use these ideas as the measure of our understanding.

There is another way to read, where the words take on a life of their own, and the rhythms and cadences open a floodgate of images and sympathies, until we feel the heartbeat of their author and sense the lifeblood of experience that they contain.

It is a way of reading that is more akin to listening to music, where the sheer power of the sound can move the hearer to tears.

This is the way we should read these words of the three great chiefs, Red Jacket, Joseph, and Seattle. Like the insistent beat of ceremonial drums, their words weave a hypnotic spell, and the passion of their vision enters into the hearts as well as the minds of their listeners.

These speeches are the songs of the spirit of great men who spoke for a great people. In their words, between their words, beneath and above their words, is the love, the faith, the anger, and the pathos of a people who believed in the ways of their ancestors and could not make these ways understood to the European settlers who were so intent upon changing them.

Today the battle is over. This continent is, at least on the surface, a distant mirror of the European continent, controlled in its shape and direction by the descendants of the Europeans who were once raw immigrants on its shores.

But the spirit of the Native people, the first people, has never died. It lives in the rocks and the forests, the rivers and the mountains. It murmurs in the brooks and whispers in the trees.

The hearts of these people were formed of the earth that we now walk, and their voice can never be silenced. The three speeches gathered here give us a chance to hear that voice again.

The selection of these particular speeches was made with care and love. I could have chosen more; I could have chosen otherwise. But these three, each imbued with its own individual genius, work together in a way that is almost transcendent in its poignancy and beauty.

Red Jacket's speech shows us the strength and faith of the traditional way, and stands like an oak against the coming storms of the European. Chief Joseph's speech takes us along on the journey of a people from free, loving, and hopeful children of the land to a fugitive remnant pursued through forests and mountains into a tragic submission on the windswept foothills of the Rockies. Chief Seattle's speech begins as an eloquent eulogy to the Indian people, but soon rises to become an admonition to us all, and a bonding together of the Indian and non-Indian into a common fate.

In the course of the three, we are carried along from the sunrise hopes of the Native peoples as they offered the hand of friendship to a new and foreign visitor, to the sunset of their dreams as this visitor grew in number and in strength and betrayed the friendship with which he had been met, to the dawning of a new era in which we all must learn the lessons of the Native people if we are to live honorably upon this land we all now share.

Readers who would wish to hear the Native American voice from other perspectives are encouraged to seek out the Classic Wisdom volumes *Native American Wisdom* and *The Soul of an Indian and Other Writings from Ohiyesa*. In *Native American Wisdom*, the Indian experience and vision is expressed in many voices from many sources. In *The Soul of an Indian*, the great Dakota thinker, Ohiyesa (also known as Charles Eastman), gives us a profoundly personal portrait of the beliefs and way of life of his people.

But for the reader who would feel the heartbeat of the Native American experience in the words and spirits of individual men, *The Wisdom of the Great Chiefs* offers an unparalleled opportunity. It is a chance to sit at the feet of the masters and to hear afresh the truths that the land and their experience granted them.

Accord these men — Red Jacket, Joseph, and Seattle — the honor they deserve. Listen silently, respectfully, and patiently, as if you are in the presence of an elder. Feel the cadences, hear the sonorities. But, most of all, open yourself to the deep spiritual truths that their words contain.

These are wise men. They have much to teach. If we listen carefully, with good heart, they may teach us. I hope so, for we, as a nation, still have much to learn.

Kent Nerburn
Bemidji, Minnesota, 1994

1

Chief Red Jacket

INTRODUCTION

The Seneca people were part of the great Iroquois federation of tribes that lived in the area we now know as upstate New York. This federation of tribes, also known as the Five Nations (or the Six Nations after the addition of the Tuscarora), was unique among Native peoples in the sophistication of its political organization. The Six Nations lived in a rough geographic line extending from the eastern edge of New York to the western. They called this territory their "long house," and each tribe had its place and its role.

The Senecas were the westernmost tribe, and were responsible for what was known as the "western door" of the long house. When a visitor or messenger came to this western door, it was the responsibility of the Senecas to assay the purpose of the visit. If it was something of little consequence, they were empowered to dispose of it in their own council. But if the subject under consideration proved to be something of importance to all the tribes of the federation, a runner was sent to call for a general meeting. The tribes then gathered and discussed the issue at hand, listening and speaking until common understanding had been reached.

It was this practice of government by council and consensus that fostered the oratorical genius of the people of the Iroquois federation. The need to discuss ideas clearly and directly, and to arrive at decisions which all could support, bred in the Iroquois an eloquence that European observers often compared to that of the Roman Senate.

It was to this tradition that Red Jacket was heir, and he undertook the task of oratorical training with extreme diligence. He studied other great speakers and their subtleties of style. He worked on musicality and nuance, and he strove to master the use of metaphor and poetic expression.

By the time he had achieved prominence in his tribe, he was capable of oratorical expression so full of nuance and poetry that government agent Horatio Jones called his oratorical talents "among the noblest that nature ever conferred upon man."

The speech quoted here was given in the summer of 1805. Its occasion was a meeting of the assembled chiefs of the Iroquois federation. They had gathered in council to hear the request of a young missionary named Cram, who had been sent among them by the Evangelical Missionary Society of Massachusetts. This society had sent missionaries before, and had met with some success. But the Indians apparently had not taken as fully to Christianity as the society had hoped. The society now hoped to establish Cram among the Iroquois so as to further their education in the Christian religion.

Cram spoke briefly, requesting only the right to follow up on the interest that certain of the Indians had shown in the Christian religion. After hearing him, the chiefs consulted for about two hours. Then Red Jacket rose and spoke.

▲▲▲

"We do not wish to destroy your religion, or to take it from you. We only want to enjoy our own."

— Chief Red Jacket, 1805

Friend and brother, it was the will of the Great Spirit that we should meet together this day. He orders all things, and He has given us a fine day for our council. He has taken His garment from before the sun and has caused it to shine with brightness upon us.

Our eyes are opened so that we see clearly. Our ears are unstopped so that we have been able to distinctly hear the words which you have spoken.

For all these favors we thank the Great Spirit and Him only.

Brother, this council fire was kindled by you. It was at your request that we came together at this time. We have listened with attention to what you have said.

You have requested us to speak our minds freely. This gives us great joy, for we now consider that we stand upright before you, and can speak

5

what we think. All have heard your voice and all speak to you now as one man. Our minds are agreed.

Brother, you say that you want an answer to your talk before you leave this place. It is right that you should have one, as you are a great distance from home, and we do not wish to detain you. But we will first look back a little, and tell you what our fathers have told us, and what we have heard from the white people.

Brother, listen to what we say.

There was a time when our forefathers owned this great island. [The Seneca, like many other tribes, refer to this continent as a "great island."] Their seats extended from the rising to the setting of the sun. The Great Spirit had made it for the use of Indians. He had created the buffalo, the deer, and other animals for food. He had made the bear and the beaver, and their skins served us for clothing. He had scattered them over the country, and had taught us how to take them. He had caused the earth to produce corn for bread.

All this He had done for His red children because He loved them.

If we had any disputes about hunting grounds, they were generally settled without the shedding of much blood. But an evil day came upon us. Your forefathers crossed the great waters and landed upon this island.

Their numbers were small. They found friends and not enemies. They told us they had fled from their own country for fear of wicked men, and had come here to enjoy their religion.

They asked for a small seat. We took pity on them, granted their request, and they sat down amongst us.

We gave them corn and meat. They gave us poison [rum] in return.

The white people, brother, had now found our country. Tidings were carried back and more came amongst us. Yet we did not fear them. We took them to be friends.

They called us brothers. We believed them and gave them a larger seat.

At length their numbers had greatly increased. They wanted more land. They wanted our country.

Our eyes were opened, and our minds became uneasy.

Wars took place. Indians were hired to fight against Indians, and many of our people were destroyed.

They also brought strong liquor among us. It was strong and powerful and has slain thousands.

Brother, our seats were once large, and yours were very small. You have now become a great people, and we have scarcely a place left to spread our blankets. You have got our country, but you are not satisfied. You want to force your religion upon us.

Brother, continue to listen.

You say that you are sent to instruct us how to worship the Great Spirit agreeably to His mind, and if we do not take hold of the religion which you white people teach we shall be unhappy hereafter.

You say that you are right, and we are lost.

How do we know this to be true?

We understand that your religion is written in a book. If it was intended for us as well, why has not the Great Spirit given it to us; and not only to us, but why did He not give to our forefathers the knowledge of that book, with the means of understanding it rightly? We know only what you tell us about it. How shall we know when to believe, being so often deceived by the white people?

Brother, you say there is but one way to worship and serve the Great Spirit. If there is but one religion, why do you white people differ so much about it? Why not all agree, as you can all read the book?

Brother, we do not understand these things.

We are told that your religion was given to your forefathers and has been handed down, father to son. We also have a religion which was given to our forefathers, and has been handed down to us, their children.

We worship in that way. It teaches us to be thankful for all the favors we receive, to love each other, and to be united. We never quarrel about religion.

Brother, the Great Spirit has made us all. But He has made a great difference between His white and red children. He has given us a different complexion and different customs. To you He has given the arts; to these He has not opened our eyes. We know these things to be true.

Since He has made so great a difference between us in other things, why may we not conclude that He has given us a different religion, according to our understanding?

The Great Spirit does right. He knows what is best for His children. We are satisfied.

Brother, we do not wish to destroy your religion, or to take it from you. We only want to enjoy our own.

Brother, you say you have not come to get our land or our money, but to enlighten our minds. I will now tell you that I have been at your meetings and saw you collecting money from the meeting.

I cannot tell you what the money was intended for, but suppose it was for your minister; and if we should conform to your way of thinking, perhaps you should want some from us.*

Brother, we are told that you have been preaching to the white people in this place. These people are our neighbors. We are acquainted with

---

*This paragraph does not appear in the first recorded edition of the speech as recorded by James D. Bemis in 1811. It does appear in later transcriptions by other authors. Its particularity and pointedness do not seem to be in keeping with the general tone of the speech, but I have chosen to leave it in, despite reservations about its authenticity.

them. We will wait a little while, and see what effect your preaching has upon them. If we find it does them good and makes them honest and less disposed to cheat Indians, we will then consider again what you have said.

Brother, you have now heard our answer to your talk, and this is all we have to say at present. As we are going to part, we will come and take you by the hand, and hope the Great Spirit will protect you on your journey, and return you safe to your friends.

▲ ▲ ▲

At the end of the speech, Red Jacket rose and approached the missionary with his hand extended. The missionary refused to take it.

2

Chief Joseph

INTRODUCTION

Chief Joseph of the Nez Perce is considered by Native and non-Native people alike as one of the greatest of all Indian leaders. "Buffalo Bill" Cody called Joseph "the greatest Indian America ever produced." Edward Curtis, who devoted much of his life to photographing the American Indian, said of Joseph, "I think he was one of the greatest men who ever lived."

Such words were not without justification. Joseph was a singular man with a deep and abiding sense of justice and an unshakable love for his people and the land to which they were born. He was unfailingly fair in his dealings with everyone he met, and unceasing in his efforts to serve the good of his people.

Joseph assumed the chieftaincy of the Nez Perce people upon the death of his father in 1871. He inherited a situation of almost impossible complexity. In 1854 the Nez Perce bands had unwillingly signed a treaty with the United States in an effort to protect their homelands. There is some question as to whether Joseph's father actually signed this treaty, but it is clear that he was radically opposed to the idea.

While this treaty had significantly reduced the size of the Nez Perce lands, it had also guaranteed their sovereignty over the land that remained. But gold had been discovered in 1860, and almost overnight entire settlements had appeared on Nez Perce land in direct violation of this treaty.

The United States had then pressured the Nez Perce to sign another treaty cutting the size of their land even further. The Nez Perce had disagreed over the wisdom of signing this new treaty, which would have diminished their lands by another 90 percent, and had dissolved their federation. Joseph's father had been among those refusing to sign. Another chief had then made the treaty with the U.S., and in this treaty had signed over the lands of Joseph's band.

Shortly afterward, Joseph assumed the chieftaincy of his band, and settlers began pouring into his land based on the conditions of the treaty his father had never signed.

Joseph, who was a supremely honorable man, found himself in the middle of a deeply troubling situation. He would not give up his homeland, which his father had sworn him to preserve, but he did not wish to do harm to the struggling white settlers who had come to his valley innocently and in good faith.

In an effort to keep his land for his people, Joseph called a council and instructed the settlers to leave. Eventually a presidential decree supported his position, but within a year the Commissioner of Indian Affairs reversed this decree without informing Joseph.

The series of events that followed eventually led Joseph to take his people, along with the other non-treaty Indians, on the famous thousand-mile flight through the rugged country of Oregon, Idaho, and Montana, in an attempt to get to Canada where they could live in peace.

The Nez Perce had never looked upon their exodus as a fight. Indeed, they fought only when necessary to facilitate their flight and to protect their elderly and children. Joseph endeavored to keep the tempers of his warriors under control, and he even helped white settlers he encountered along the way.

But the flight became a major media event throughout the United States. The government was not about to allow a group of Indian refugees traveling with elderly, women, and infants to escape from the massed forces of the U.S. military.

On October 5, 1877, only forty miles from the freedom of Canada, the Nez Perce were faced with a heart-rending decision. The military had once again surrounded them. The warriors determined that they could elude capture, but to do so would require them to leave their elderly, wounded, and children behind. This they would not do.

And so it was, after discussing the matter with the other Nez Perce chief, that Joseph rode forth under the early winter sky of the Bear Paw foothills and spoke his now-famous words to the representatives of the U.S. military: "From where the sun now stands, I will fight no more forever."

He did not do this as a surrender. He felt confident that reinforcements from Sitting Bull were on the way, and that he could prevail if he waited. But he had been promised by the U.S. general that if both sides laid down their arms, the Nez Perce could return to their home. In Joseph's mind, it had been the offer of an armistice, and he had accepted it because the 184 women and 147 children with him were freezing and starving.

But the government soon failed to keep the promise of its general. Joseph and his Nez Perce were moved to North Dakota, and then to Kansas, where an epidemic of malaria ravaged what remained of his people.

It was against this backdrop that Joseph came to Washington to plead the cause of his people. On January 14, 1879, barely a year after he had submitted his people to the U.S. military on that raw and blustery October day, Joseph stood in Lincoln Hall in Washington, D.C., before an assembly of congressmen, diplomats, and dignitaries, and delivered the following speech.

We cannot know the exact words he spoke that evening; the version that has come down to us was published several months later in a distinguished periodical, *The North American Review*. But we can surmise, from the version we do have, that in those two hours he painted one of the most poignant portraits of the Indian experience that has ever been voiced by any American.

The speech is often quoted, but seldom reproduced in its entirety due to its length. But that length is deceptive. Joseph speaks in simple, straightforward sentences that lead us relentlessly through the events that reduced his people from a peaceful, prosperous nation to a disease-ridden remnant living in squalor, without food or medicine, on inhospitable lands.

His logic is unassailable; his contained passion, riveting. He speaks with candor and clarity, sparing no one in the unflinching honesty of his narrative. It is a speech of pathos and power, anger and dignity. Perhaps more than any other, this speech embodies the experience of the Native American after the arrival of the European on North American soil.

▲ ▲ ▲

"The earth is the mother of all people, and all people should have equal rights upon it."

— Chief Joseph, 1879

My friends, I have been asked to show you my heart. I am glad to have a chance to do so. I want the white people to understand my people.

Some of you think an Indian is like a wild animal. This is a great mistake. I will tell you all about our people, and then you can judge whether an Indian is a man or not.

I believe much trouble would be saved if we opened our hearts more. I will tell you in my way how the Indian sees things. The white man has more words to tell you how they look to him, but it does not require many words to speak the truth.

What I have to say will come straight from my heart, and I will speak with a straight tongue. The Great Spirit is looking at me, and will hear me.

My name is In-mut-too-yah-lat-lat [Thunder Traveling over Mountains]. I am chief of the Wal-lam-wat-kin band of the Chute-pa-lu, or Nez

Perce. I was born in eastern Oregon, thirty-eight winters ago.

My father was chief before me. When a young man, he was called Joseph by Mr. Spaulding, a missionary. He died a few years ago. He left a good name on earth. He advised me well for my people.

Our fathers gave us many laws, which they had learned from their fathers. These laws were good. They told us to treat all men as they treated us, that we should never be the first to break a bargain, that it was a disgrace to tell a lie, that we should speak only the truth, that it was a shame for one man to take from another his wife or his property without paying for it.

We were taught to believe that the Great Spirit sees and hears everything, and that He never forgets; that hereafter He will give every man a spirit-home according to his deserts: If he has been a good man, he will have a good home; if he has been a bad man, he will have a bad home.

This I believe, and all my people believe the same.

We did not know there were other people besides the Indian until about one hundred winters ago, when some men with white faces came to our country. They brought many things with them to trade for furs and skins. They brought tobacco, which was new to us. They brought guns with flint stones on them, which frightened our women and children. Our people could not talk with these white-faced men, but they used signs which all people understand.

These men were called Frenchmen, and they called our people "Nez Perce," because they wore rings in their noses for ornaments. Although very few of our people wear them now, we are still called by the same name.

These French trappers said a great many things to our fathers, which have been planted in our hearts. Some were good for us, but some were bad.

Our people were divided in opinion about these men. Some thought they taught more bad than good. An Indian respects a brave man, but he despises a coward. He loves a straight tongue, but he hates a forked tongue. The French trappers told us some truths and some lies.

The first white men of your people who came to our country were named Lewis and Clark. They also brought many things that our people had never seen. They talked straight, and our people gave them a great feast as a proof that their hearts were friendly.

These men were very kind. They made presents to our chiefs and our people made presents to them. We had a great many horses, of which we gave them what they needed, and they gave us guns and tobacco in return.

All the Nez Perce made friends with Lewis and Clark, and agreed to let them pass through their country, and never to make war on white men. This promise the Nez Perce have never broken. No white man can accuse them of bad faith and speak with a straight tongue. It has always been the pride of the Nez Perce that they were the friends of the white men.

When my father was a young man there came to our country a white man [Rev. Henry H. Spaulding] who talked spirit law. He won the affections of our people because he spoke good things to them. At first he did not say anything about white men wanting to settle on our lands. Nothing was said about that until about twenty winters ago, when a number of white people came into our country and built houses and made farms.

At first our people made no complaint. They thought there was room enough for all to live in peace, and they were learning many things from the white men that seemed to be good.

But we soon found that the white men were growing rich very fast, and were greedy to possess everything the Indian had. My father was the first to see through the schemes of the white men, and he warned his tribe to be careful about trading with them. He had suspicion of men who seemed anxious to make money.

I was a boy then, but I remember well my father's caution. He had sharper eyes than the rest of our people.

Next there came a white officer [Governor Isaac Stevens of the Washington Territory], who invited all the Nez Perce to a treaty council. After the council was opened he made known his heart. He said there were a great many white people in our country, and many more would come; that he wanted the land marked out so that the Indians and the white men could be separated. If they were to live in peace it was necessary, he said, that the Indians should have a country set apart for them, and in that country they must stay.

My father, who represented his band, refused to have anything to do with the council, because he wished to be a free man. He claimed that no man owned any part of the earth, and a man could not sell what he did not own.

Mr. Spaulding took hold of my father's arm and said, "Come and sign the treaty."

My father pushed him away, and said, "Why do you ask me to sign away my country? It is your business to talk to us about spirit matters and not to talk to us about parting with our land."

Governor Stevens urged my father to sign his treaty, but he refused. "I will not sign your paper," he said. "You go where you please, so do I. You are not a child. I am no child. I can think for myself. No man can think for me. I have no home other than this. I will not give it up to any man. My people would have no home. Take away your paper. I will not touch it with my hand."

My father left the council. Some of the chiefs of the other bands of the Nez Perce signed the treaty, and then Governor Stevens gave them presents of blankets. My father cautioned his people to take no presents, for "after a while," he said, "they will claim that you have accepted pay for your country."

Since that time four bands of the Nez Perce have received annuities from the United States. My father was invited to many councils, and they tried hard to make him sign the treaty, but he was firm as the rock, and would not sign away his home. His refusal caused a difference among the Nez Perce.

Eight years later [1863] was the next treaty council. A chief called Lawyer, because he was a great talker, took the lead in the council, and sold nearly all the Nez Perce country.

My father was not there. He said to me: "When you go into council with the white man, always remember your country. Do not give it away. The white man will cheat you out of your home. I have taken no pay from the United States. I have never sold our land."

In this treaty Lawyer acted without authority from our band. He had no right to sell the Wallowa country. [The Wallowa country, which means "the land of winding water," is in the northeastern part of what is now the state of Oregon. It is the ancestral home of Joseph's band of the Nez

Perce.] That had always belonged to my father's own people, and the other bands had never disputed our right to it. No other Indians ever claimed Wallowa.

In order to have all people understand how much land we owned, my father planted poles around it and said, "Inside is the home of my people. The white man may take the land outside. Inside this boundary all our people were born. It circles around the graves of our fathers, and we will never give up these graves to any man."

The United States claimed they had bought all the Nez Perce country outside the Lapwai Reservation from Lawyer and other chiefs. But we continued to live on this land in peace until eight years ago, when white men began to come inside the boundaries my father had set.

We warned them against this great wrong, but they would not leave our land, and some bad blood was raised. The white men represented that we were going upon the warpath. They reported many things that were false.

The United States government again asked for a treaty council. My father had become blind and feeble. He could no longer speak for his people. It was then that I took my father's place as chief. In this council I made my first speech to white men.

I said to the agent who held the council: "I did not want to come to this council, but I came hoping that we could save blood. The white man has no right to come here and take our country. We have never accepted any presents from the government. Neither Lawyer nor any other chief had authority to sell this land. It has always belonged to my people. It came unclouded to them from our fathers, and we will defend this land as long as a drop of Indian blood warms the hearts of our men."

The agent said he had orders from the Great White Chief at Washington for us to go upon the Lapwai Reservation, and that if we obeyed, he would help us in many ways.

"You must move to the agency," he said.

I answered him, "I will not. I do not need your help. We have plenty, and we are contented and happy if the white man will let us alone. The reservation is too small for so many people with all their stock. You can keep your presents. We can go to your towns and pay for all we need. We have plenty of horses and cattle to sell, and we won't have any help from you. We are free now; we can go where we please. Our fathers were born here. Here they lived, here they died, here are their graves. We will never leave them."

The agent went away and we had peace for a little while.

Soon after this my father sent for me. I saw he was dying. I took his hand in mine. He said, "My son, my body is returning to my mother earth, and my spirit is going very soon to see the Great Spirit Chief. When I am gone, think of your country. You are the chief of these people. They look to you to guide them. Always remember that your father never sold this country. You must stop your ears whenever you are asked to sign a treaty selling your home. A few years more, and white men will be all around you. They have their eyes on this land. My son, never forget my dying words. This country holds your father's body. Never sell the bones of your father and mother."

I pressed my father's hand and told him I would protect his grave with my life. My father smiled and passed away to the spirit land.

I buried him in that beautiful valley of winding waters. I love that land more than all the rest of the world. A man who would not love his father's grave is worse than a wild animal.

For a short time we lived quietly. But this could not last. White men had found gold in the mountains around the land of winding water. They stole many horses from us, and we could not get them back because we were Indians.

The white men told lies for each other. They drove off a great many of our cattle. Some white men branded our young cattle so they could claim them.

We had no friend who would plead our cause before the law councils. It seemed to me that some of the white men in Wallowa were doing these things on purpose to get up a war. They knew that we were not strong enough to fight them.

I labored hard to avoid trouble and bloodshed. We gave up some of our country to the white men, thinking that then we could have peace.

We were mistaken. The white man would not let us alone.

We could have avenged our wrongs many times, but we did not. Whenever the government has asked us to help them against other Indians, we have never refused. When the white men were few and we were strong, we could have killed them all off, but the Nez Perce wished to live at peace.

If we have not done so, we have not been to blame. I believe that the old treaty has never been correctly reported. If we ever owned the land we own it still, for we never sold it.

In the treaty councils the commissioners have claimed that our country had been sold to the government. Suppose a white man should come to me and say, "Joseph, I like your horses, and I want to buy them."

I say to him, "No, my horses suit me. I will not sell them."

Then he goes to my neighbor and says to him, "Joseph has some good horses. I want to buy them, but he refuses to sell."

My neighbor answers, "Pay me the money, and I will sell you Joseph's horses."

The white man returns to me and says, "Joseph, I have bought your horses, and you must let me have them."

If we sold our lands to the government, this is the way they were bought.

On account of the treaty made by the other bands of the Nez Perce, the white men claimed my lands. We were troubled greatly by white men crowding over the line. Some of these were good men, and we lived on peaceful terms with them. But they were not all good.

Nearly every year the agent came over from Lapwai and ordered us on to the reservation. We always replied that we were satisfied to live in Wallowa. We were careful to refuse presents or annuities which he offered.

Through all the years since the white men came to Wallowa, we have been threatened and taunted by them and the treaty Nez Perce. They have given us no rest.

We have had a few good friends among white men, and they have always advised my people to bear these taunts without fighting. Our young men were quick-tempered, and I have had great trouble in keeping them from doing rash things.

I have carried a heavy load on my back ever since I was a boy. I learned then that we were but few, while the white men were many, and that we could not hold our own with them.

We were like deer. They were like grizzly bears.

We had a small country. Their country was large.

We were contented to let things remain as the Great Spirit Chief made them. They were not, and would change the rivers and the mountains if they did not suit them.

Year after year we have been threatened, but no war was made upon my people until General Howard came to our country two years ago and told us he was the white war-chief of all that country. He said, "I have a great many soldiers at my back. I am going to bring them up here, and then I will talk to you again. I will not let white men laugh at me the next time I come. The country belongs to the government, and I intend to make you go upon the reservation."

I remonstrated with him against bringing more soldiers to the Nez Perce country. He had one house full of troops all the time at Fort Lapwai.

The next spring the agent at Umatilla agency sent an Indian runner to tell me to meet General Howard at Walla Walla. I could not go myself, but I sent my brother and five other head men to meet him, and they had a long talk.

General Howard said, "You have talked straight, and it is all right. You can stay in Wallowa."

He insisted that my brother should go with him to Fort Lapwai. When the party arrived there General Howard sent out runners and called all the Indians in to a grand council. I was in that council.

I said to General Howard, "We are ready to listen."

He answered that he would not talk then, but would hold a council next day, when he would talk plainly.

I said to General Howard, "I am ready to talk today. I have been in a great many councils, but I am no wiser. We are all sprung from a woman, although we are unlike in many things. We cannot be made over again. You are as you were made, and as you were made you can remain. We are just as we were made by the Great Spirit, and you cannot change us. Then why should children of one mother and one father quarrel? Why should one try to cheat the other? I do not believe that the Great Spirit Chief gave one kind of men the right to tell another kind of men what they must do."

General Howard replied, "You deny my authority, do you? You want to dictate to me, do you?"

Then one of my chiefs — Too-hool-hool-suit — rose in the council and said to General Howard, "The Great Spirit Chief made the world as it is, and as He wanted it, and He made a part of it for us to live upon. I do not see where you get authority to say that we shall not live where He placed us."

General Howard lost his temper and said, "Shut up! I don't want to hear any more of such talk. The law says you shall go upon the reservation to live, and I want you to do so. But you persist in disobeying the law. If you do not move, I will take the matter into my own hand and make you suffer for your disobedience."

Too-hool-hool-suit answered, "Who are you, that you should ask us to talk, and then tell me I shan't talk? Are you the Great Spirit? Did you make the world? Did you make the sun? Did you make the rivers to run for us to drink? Did you make the grass to grow? Did you make all these things, that you talk to us as though we were boys? If you did, then you have the right to talk as you do."

General Howard replied, "You are an impudent fellow, and I will put you in the guard house," and then ordered a soldier to arrest him.

Too-hool-hool-suit made no resistance. He asked General Howard, "Is that your order? I don't care. I have expressed my heart to you. I have nothing to take back. I have spoken for my country. You can arrest me, but you cannot change me or make me take back what I have said."

The soldiers came forward and seized my friend and took him to the guard house. My men whispered among themselves whether they should let this thing be done.

I counseled them to submit. I knew if we resisted that all the white men present, including General Howard, would be killed in a moment, and we would be blamed. If I had said nothing, General Howard would never have given another unjust order against my men.

I saw the danger, and while they dragged

Too-hool-hool-suit to prison, I arose and said, "I am going to talk now. I don't care whether you arrest me or not."

I turned to my people and said, "The arrest of Too-hool-hool-suit was wrong, but we will not resent the insult. We were invited to this council to express our hearts, and we have done so." Too-hool-hool-suit was prisoner for five days before he was released.

The council broke up for that day. On the next morning General Howard came to my lodge and invited me to go with him and White Bird and Looking Glass to look for land for my people.

As we rode along we came to some good land that was already occupied by Indians and white people. General Howard, pointing to this land, said, "If you will come on to the reservation, I will give you these lands and move these people off."

I replied, "No. It would be wrong to disturb these people. I have no right to take their homes. I have never taken what did not belong to me. I will not now."

We rode all day upon the reservation, and found no good land unoccupied. I have been informed by men who do not lie that General Howard sent a letter that night telling the soldiers at Walla Walla to go to Wallowa valley and drive us out upon our return home.

In the council, next day, General Howard informed me, in a haughty spirit, that he would give my people thirty days to go back home, collect all their stock, and move onto the reservation, saying, "If you are not here in that time, I shall consider that you want to fight, and will send my soldiers to drive you on."

I said, "War can be avoided, and it ought to be avoided. I want no war. My people have always been the friends of the white man. Why are you in such a hurry? I cannot get ready to move in thirty days. Our stock is scattered, and the Snake River is very high. Let us wait until fall. Then the river will be low. We want time to hunt up our stock and gather supplies for winter."

General Howard replied, "If you let the time run over one day, the soldiers will be there to drive you onto the reservation, and all your cattle and horses outside of the reservation at that time will fall into the hands of the white men."

I knew I had never sold my country, and that I had no land in Lapwai. But I did not want bloodshed. I did not want my people killed. I did not want anybody killed.

Some of my people had been murdered by white men, and the white murderers were never punished for it. I told General Howard about this, and again said I wanted no war. I wanted the people who lived upon the lands I was to occupy at Lapwai to have time to gather their harvest.

I said in my heart that, rather than have war, I would give up my country. I would give up my father's grave. I would give up everything rather than have the blood of white men upon the hands of my people.

General Howard refused to allow me more than thirty days to move my people and their stock. I am sure that he began to prepare for war at once.

When I returned to Wallowa I found my people very much excited upon discovering that the soldiers were already in the Wallowa valley. We held a council and decided to move immediately, to avoid bloodshed.

Too-hool-hool-suit, who felt outraged by his imprisonment, talked for war, and made many of my young men willing to fight rather than be driven like dogs from the land where they were born. He declared that blood alone would wash out the disgrace General Howard had put upon him. It required a strong heart to stand up against such talk, but I urged my people to be quiet, and not to begin a war.

We gathered all the stock we could find, and made an attempt to move. We left many of our horses and cattle in Wallowa, and we lost several hundred in crossing the river. All of my people succeeded in getting across in safety.

Many of the Nez Perce came together in Rocky Canyon to hold a grand council. I went with all my people. This council lasted ten days. There was a great deal of war talk, and a great deal of excitement. There was one young brave present whose father had been killed by a white man five years before. This man's blood was bad against white men, and he left the council calling for revenge.

Again I counseled peace, and I thought the danger was past.

We had not complied with General Howard's order because we could not, but we intended to do so as soon as possible. I was leaving the council to kill beef for my family when news came that the young man whose father had been killed had gone out with several other hot-blooded young braves and killed four white men.

He rode up to the council and shouted, "Why do you sit here like women? The war has begun already."

I was deeply grieved. All the lodges were moved except my brother's and my own. I saw clearly that the war was upon us when I learned that my young men had been secretly buying ammunition. I heard then that Too-hool-hool-suit, who had been imprisoned by General Howard, had succeeded in organizing a war party.

I knew that their acts would involve all my people. I saw that the war could not be prevented. The time had passed.

I counseled peace from the beginning. I knew that we were too weak to fight the United States. We had many grievances, but I knew that war would bring more.

We had good white friends, who advised us against taking the war path. My friend and brother, Mr. Chapman, who has been with us since the surrender, told us just how the war would end. Mr. Chapman took sides against us, and helped General Howard. I do not blame him for doing so. He tried hard to prevent bloodshed.

We hoped the white settlers would not join the soldiers. Before the war commenced we had discussed this matter all over, and many of my people were in favor of warning them that if they took no part against us they should not be molested in the event of war being begun by General Howard.

This plan was voted down in the war council.

There were bad men among my people who had quarreled with white men, and they talked of their wrongs until they roused all the bad hearts in the council. Still, I could not believe they would begin the war.

I know that my young men did a great wrong, but I ask, "Who was first to blame?" They had been insulted a thousand times. Their fathers and brothers had been killed. Their mothers and wives had been disgraced. They had been driven to madness by whiskey sold to them by white men. They had been told by General Howard that all their horses and cattle which they had been unable to drive out of Wallowa were to fall into the hands of white men. And, added to all this, they were homeless and desperate.

I would have given my own life if I could have undone the killing of white men by my people.

I blame my young men and I blame the white men. I blame General Howard for not giving my people time to get their stock away from Wallowa. I do not acknowledge that he had the right to order me to leave Wallowa at any time. I deny that either my father or myself ever sold that land. It is still our land. It may never again be our home, but my father sleeps there, and I love it as I love my mother. I left there hoping to avoid bloodshed.

If General Howard had given me plenty of time to gather up my stock, and treated Too-hool-hool-suit as a man should be treated, there would have been no war.

My friends among white men have blamed me for the war. I am not to blame. When my young men began the killing, my heart was hurt. Although I did not justify them, I remembered all the insults I had endured, and my blood was on fire. Still, I would have taken my people to the buffalo country without fighting if possible. I could see no other way to avoid a war.

We moved over to White Bird Creek, sixteen miles away, and there encamped, intending to collect our stock before leaving. But the soldiers attacked us, and the first battle was fought.

We numbered in that battle sixty men, and the soldiers a hundred. The fight lasted but a few minutes, when the soldiers retreated before us for twelve miles. They lost thirty-three killed, and had seven wounded.

When an Indian fights, he only shoots to kill. But soldiers shoot at random. None of the soldiers were scalped. We do not believe in scalping, nor in killing wounded men. Soldiers do not kill many Indians unless they are wounded and left upon the battle field. Then they kill Indians.

Seven days after the first battle, General Howard arrived in the Nez Perce country, bringing seven hundred more soldiers. It was now war in earnest.

We crossed the Salmon River, hoping General Howard would follow. We were not disappointed. He did follow us, and we got back between him and his supplies, and cut him off for three days.

He sent out two companies to open the way. We attacked them, killing one officer, two guides, and ten men.

We withdrew, hoping the soldiers would follow. But they had got enough fighting for that day. They entrenched themselves, and next day we attacked them again. The battle lasted all day, and was renewed next morning. We killed four and wounded seven or eight.

About this time General Howard found out that we were in his rear. Five days later he attacked us with three hundred and fifty soldiers and settlers. We had two hundred and fifty warriors.

The fight lasted twenty-seven hours. We lost four killed and several wounded. General Howard's loss was twenty-nine men killed and sixty wounded.

The following day the soldiers charged upon us, and we retreated with our families and stock a few miles, leaving eighty lodges to fall into General Howard's hands.

Finding that we were outnumbered, we retreated to the Bitterroot valley. Here another body of soldiers came upon us and demanded our surrender.

We refused.

They said, "You cannot get by us."

We answered, "We are going by you without fighting if you will let us. But we are going by you anyhow."

We then made a treaty with these soldiers. We agreed not to molest anyone, and they agreed that we might pass through the Bitterroot country in peace.

We bought provisions and traded stock with the white men there.

We understood that there was to be no more war. We intended to go peaceably to the buffalo country, and leave the question of returning to our country to be settled afterward.

With this understanding, we traveled on for four days. And, thinking that the trouble was all over, we stopped and prepared tent poles to take with us.

We started again, and at the end of two days saw three white men passing our camp. Thinking that peace had been made, we did not molest them. We could have killed them or taken them prisoners, but we did not suspect them of being spies, which they were.

That night the soldiers surrounded our camp. About daybreak one of my men went out to look after his horses. The soldiers saw him and shot him down like a coyote.

I have since learned that these soldiers were not those we had left behind. They had come upon us from another direction.

The new white war chief's name was Gibbon. He charged upon us while some of my people were still asleep. We had a hard fight. Some of my men crept around and attacked the soldiers from the rear. In this battle we lost nearly all our lodges, but we finally drove General Gibbon back.

Finding that he was not able to capture us, he sent to his camp a few miles away for his big guns [cannons]. But my men had captured them and all the ammunition.

We damaged the big guns all we could, and carried away the powder and the lead.

In the fight with General Gibbon we lost fifty women and children and thirty fighting men. We remained long enough to bury our dead. The Nez Perce never make war on women and children. We could have killed a great many women and children while the war lasted, but we would feel ashamed to do so cowardly an act.

We never scalp our enemies. But when General Howard came up and joined General Gibbon, their Indian scouts dug up our dead and scalped them. I have been told that General Howard did not order this great shame to be done.

We retreated as rapidly as we could toward the buffalo country. After six days General Howard came close to us, and we went out and attacked him, and captured nearly all his horses and mules. We then marched on to the Yellowstone Basin.

On the way we captured one white man and two white women. We released them at the end of three days. They were treated kindly. The women were not insulted. Can the white soldiers tell me of one time when Indian women were taken prisoners and held three days, and then released without being insulted? Were the Nez Perce women who fell into the hands of General Howard's soldiers treated with as much respect? I deny that a Nez Perce was ever guilty of such a crime.

A few days later we captured two more white men. One of them stole a horse and escaped. We gave the other a poor horse and told him he was free.

Nine days' march brought us to the mouth of Clark's Fork of the Yellowstone. We did not know what had become of General Howard, but we supposed that he had sent for more horses and mules.

He did not come up, but another new war chief [General Sturgis] attacked us. We held him in check while we moved all our women and children and stock out of danger, leaving a few men to cover our retreat.

Several days passed, and we heard nothing of General Howard, or Gibbon, or Sturgis. We had repulsed each in turn, and began to feel secure, when another army, under General Miles, struck us. This was the fourth army, each of which outnumbered our fighting force, that we had encountered within sixty days.

We had no knowledge of General Miles's army until a short time before he made a charge upon us, cutting our camp in two and capturing nearly all of our horses.

About seventy men, myself among them, were cut off. My little daughter, twelve years old, was with me. I gave her a rope and told her to catch a horse and join the others who were cut off from the camp. I have not seen her since, but I have learned that she is alive and well.

I thought of my wife and children, who were now surrounded by soldiers, and I resolved to go to them or die.

With a prayer in my mouth to the Great Spirit Chief who rules above, I dashed unarmed through the line of soldiers. It seemed to me that there were guns on every side, before and behind me.

My clothes were cut to pieces and my horse was wounded, but I was unharmed. As I reached the door of my lodge, my wife handed me my rifle, saying, "Here's your gun. Fight!"

The soldiers kept up a continuous fire.

Six of my men were killed in one spot near me. Ten or twelve soldiers charged into our camp and got possession of two lodges, killing three Nez Perce and losing three of their men, who fell inside our lines.

I called my men to drive them back.

We fought at close range, not more than twenty steps apart, and drove the soldiers back upon their main line, leaving their dead in our hands.

We secured their arms and ammunition. We lost, the first day and night, eighteen men and three women. General Miles lost twenty-six killed and forty wounded.

The following day General Miles sent a messenger into my camp under protection of a white flag. I sent my friend Yellow Bull to meet him.

Yellow Bull understood the messenger to say that General Miles wished me to consider the situation, that he did not want to kill my people unnecessarily. Yellow Bull understood this to be a demand for me to surrender and save blood.

Upon reporting this message to me, Yellow Bull said he wondered whether General Miles was in earnest. I sent him back with my answer, that I had made up my mind, but would think about it and send word soon.

A little later he sent some Cheyenne scouts with another message. I went out to meet them.

They said they believed that General Miles was sincere and really wanted peace.

I walked to General Miles's tent. He met me and we shook hands. He said, "Come, let us sit down by the fire and talk this matter over."

I remained with him all night. Next morning Yellow Bull came over to see if I was alive, and why I did not return.

General Miles would not let me leave the tent to see my friend alone.

Yellow Bull said to me, "They have got you in their power, and I am afraid they will never let you go again. I have an officer in our camp, and I will hold him until they let you go free."

I said, "I do not know what they mean to do with me, but if they kill me you must not kill the officer. It will do no good to avenge my death by killing him."

Yellow Bull returned to my camp.

I did not make any agreement that day with General Miles. The battle was renewed while I was with him. I was very anxious about my people. I knew that we were near Sitting Bull's camp in King George's land, and I thought maybe the Nez Perce who had escaped would return with assistance. No great damage was done to either party during the night.

On the following morning I returned to my camp by agreement, meeting the officer who had been held a prisoner in my camp at the flag of truce.

My people were divided about surrendering. We could have escaped from Bear Paw Mountain if we had left our wounded, old men, and children behind. We were unwilling to do this. We had never heard of a wounded Indian recovering while in the hands of white men.

On the evening of the fourth day, General Howard came in with a small escort, together with my friend Chapman. We could now talk understandingly.

General Miles said to me in plain words, "If you will come out and give up your arms, I will spare your lives and send you to your reservation." I do not know what passed between General Miles and General Howard.

I could not bear to see my wounded men and women suffer any longer. We had lost enough already.

General Miles had promised that we might return to our own country with what stock we had left. I thought we could start again. I believed General Miles, or I never would have surrendered.

I have heard that he has been censured for making the promise to return us to Lapwai. He could not have made any other terms with me at that time. I would have held him in check until my friends came to my assistance, and then neither of the generals nor their soldiers would have ever left Bear Paw Mountain alive.

On the fifth day I went to General Miles and gave up my gun, and said, "From where the sun now stands I will fight no more."

My people needed rest. We wanted peace.

I was told we could go with General Miles to Tongue River and stay there until spring, when we would be sent back to our country.

Finally it was decided that we were about to be taken to Tongue River. We had nothing to say about it. After our arrival at Tongue River, General Miles received orders to take us to Bismarck. The reason given was that subsistence would be cheaper there.

General Miles opposed this order. He said, "You must not blame me. I have endeavored to keep my word, but the chief who is over me has given the order, and I must obey it or resign. That would do you no good. Some other officer would carry out the order."

I believe General Miles would have kept his word if he could have done so. I do not blame him for what we have suffered since the surrender. I do not know who is to blame. We gave up all our horses — over eleven hundred — and all our saddles — over one hundred — and we have not heard from them since. Someone has got our horses.

General Miles turned my people over to another soldier, and we were taken to Bismarck.

Captain Johnson, who now had charge of us, received an order to take us to Leavenworth. At Leavenworth we were placed on a low river bottom, with no water except river water to drink and cook with.

We had always lived in a healthy country, where the mountains were high and the water was cold and clear. Many of my people sickened and died, and we buried them in this strange land.

I cannot tell how much my heart suffered for my people while at Leavenworth. The Great Spirit Chief who rules above seemed to be looking some other way, and did not see what was being done to my people.

During the hot days we received notice that we were to be moved farther away from our own country. We were not asked if we were willing to go.

We were ordered to get into railroad cars. Three of my people died on the way to Baxter Springs [Kansas]. It was worse to die there than to die fighting in the mountains.

We were moved from Baxter Springs to the Indian Territory, and set down without our lodges. We had but little medicine, and we were nearly all sick.

Seventy of my people have died since we moved there.

We have had a great many visitors who have talked many ways.

Some of the chiefs from Washington came to see us, and selected land for us to live upon. We have not moved to that land, for it is not a good place to live.

The Commissioner Chief [E. A. Hayt] came to see us. I told him, as I told everyone, that I expected General Miles's word would be carried out.

He said it could not be done; that white men now lived in my country and all the land was taken up; that if I returned to Wallowa, I could not live in peace; that law-papers were out against my young men who began the war; and that the government could not protect my people.

This talk fell like a heavy stone upon my heart.

I saw that I could not gain anything by talking to him. Other law chiefs came to see me and said they would help me get a healthy country.

I did not know who to believe. The white men have too many chiefs. They do not understand each other. They do not all talk alike.

The Commissioner Chief invited me to go with him and hunt for a better home than we have now. I like the land we found [west of the Osage Reservation] better than any place I have seen in that country.

But it is not a healthy land. There are no mountains and rivers. The water is warm. It is not a good country for stock.

I do not believe my people can live there. I am afraid they will all die. The Indians who occupy that country are all dying off. I promised Chief Hayt to go there and do the best I could until the government got ready to make good General Miles's word. I was not satisfied, but I could not help myself.

Then the Inspector Chief [General McNeill] came to my camp and we had a long talk. He said I ought to have a home in the mountain country north, and that he would write a letter to the Great Chief at Washington. Again the hope of seeing the mountains of Idaho and Oregon grew up in my heart.

At last I was granted permission to come to Washington and bring my friend Yellow Bull and our interpreter with me. I am glad we came. I have shaken hands with a great many friends.

But there are some things I want to know which no one seems able to explain.

I cannot understand how the government sends a man out to fight us, as it did General Miles, and then breaks his word. Such a government has something wrong about it.

I cannot understand why so many chiefs are allowed to talk so many different ways, and promise so many different things. I have seen the Great

Father Chief [president], the next Great Chief [secretary of the Interior], the Commissioner Chief [Hayt], the Law Chief [General Butler], and many other law chiefs [congressmen], and they all say they are my friends, and that I shall have justice. But while their mouths all talk right I do not understand why nothing has been done for my people.

I have heard talk and talk, but nothing is done. Good words do not last long unless they amount to something.

Words do not pay for my dead people. They do not pay for my country, now overrun by white men. They do not protect my father's grave. They do not pay for all my horses and cattle.

Good words will not give me back my children. Good words will not make good the promise of your War Chief General Miles. Good words will not give my people good health and stop them from dying. Good words will not get my people a home where they can live in peace and take care of themselves.

I am tired of talk that comes to nothing.

It makes my heart sick when I remember all the good words and the broken promises.

There has been too much talking by men who had no right to talk. Too many misrepresentations have been made; too many misunderstandings have come up between the white men about the Indians.

If the white man wants to live in peace with the Indian he can live in peace. There need be no trouble. Treat all men alike. Give them the same law. Give them all an even chance to live and grow.

All men were made by the same Great Spirit Chief. They are all brothers. The earth is the mother of all people, and all people should have equal rights upon it.

You might as well expect the rivers to run backward as that any man who was born a free man should be contented when penned up and denied liberty to go where he pleases. If you tie a horse to a stake, do you expect he will grow fat? If you pen an Indian up on a small spot of earth and compel him to stay there, he will not be contented, nor will he grow and prosper.

I have asked some of the great white chiefs where they get their authority to say to the Indian that he shall stay in one place, while he sees white men going where they please. They cannot tell me.

I only ask of the government to be treated as all other men are treated. If I cannot go to my own home, let me have a home in some country where my people will not die so fast.

I would like to go to the Bitterroot valley. There my people would be healthy; where they are now, they are dying. Three have died since I left my camp to come to Washington.

When I think of our condition my heart is heavy. I see men of my race treated as outlaws and driven from country to country, or shot down like animals.

I know that my race must change. We cannot hold our own with the white men as we are. We only ask an even chance to live as other men live.

We ask to be recognized as men. We ask that the same law shall work alike on all men. If the Indian breaks the law, punish him by the law. If the white man breaks the law, punish him also.

Let me be a free man — free to travel, free to stop, free to work, free to trade where I choose, free to choose my own teachers, free to follow the religion of my fathers, free to think and talk and act for myself — and I will obey every law, or submit to the penalty.

When the white man treats an Indian as they treat each other, then we will have no more wars. We shall all be alike — brothers of one father and one mother, with one sky above us and one government for all.

Then the Great Spirit Chief who rules above will smile upon this land, and send rain to wash out the bloody spots made by brothers' hands from the face of the earth.

For this time the Indian race are waiting and praying.

I hope that no more groans of wounded men and women will ever go to the ear of the Great Spirit Chief above, and that all people may be one people.

In-mut-too-yah-lat-lat has spoken for his people.

▲ ▲ ▲

Joseph died in 1904, twenty-five years after delivering this speech. He was still confined on a reservation far from his ancestral homeland.

Dr. E. H. Latham, the agency physician who had attended Joseph for the last fourteen years of his life, explained the cause of death simply: "Chief Joseph died of a broken heart. . . ."

3

Chief Seattle

INTRODUCTION

No speech ever given by an Indian leader has been so widely quoted, or so widely revered, as the speech given by Chief Seattle of the Suquamish people in 1853.

Its setting was a cold December day on the shores of the area the Indians called "the Whulge," and the white people called Puget Sound in what is now the state of Washington. Over a thousand Indians had gathered to await the arrival of a ship carrying Isaac Stevens, who had recently been appointed by President Pierce to serve as the governor of the newly created Washington Territory. The Indians knew little about

Stevens, but they knew that he carried their fate in his hands. Their vigil on the wintry shores was as much an act of curiosity as a gesture of respect.

When the ship carrying Stevens arrived, the new governor stepped on shore without ceremony. He was a diminutive man, brusque in his manner and direct in his approach to people and problems. He had been appointed to facilitate the settling of the area, and to do so he had to remove the native inhabitants so they would not impede the progress of the white settlers. He was anxious to get on with the matter.

He began speaking in rapid-fire sentences that even the interpreters were hard pressed to understand. Little was clear to the Indian people, except that this man intended to remove them from their ancestral lands and place them on prison plots of earth he called "reservations."

When Stevens was done speaking, the Indians turned toward Chief Seattle. He had long been recognized as the leader of the allied tribes of the Whulge. It was only natural that he should speak for them all.

Seattle was a thoughtful man. Though he had achieved his early reputation by his military prowess, it had always been his conviction that talk toward peace was preferable to actions toward war. When the whites had begun arriving in the 1830s, he had welcomed them, and even converted to their Christian religion. While other tribes had banded together to resist this foreign encroachment, Seattle had kept his people of the Whulge as far from battle as he could.

Even after 1851, when the emigration across the Oregon Trail had brought legions of settlers into the Northwest, Seattle had continued to believe that the bounty of the land would provide for all, and he had continued to help the settlers establish a life on his beloved Whulge.

But as the years had progressed, and white settlement had increased, Seattle had come to realize that the two cultures could not easily coexist. Indian willingness to share the land had been interpreted by the settlers as an offer of permanent ownership. The Indian tradition of gift-giving was being exploited by the more commerce-minded whites who were intent upon advantage, not fairness and honor. Even the white justice system was encroaching on the Indian ways: Disagreements between Indians were being adjudicated by the white government, even though the Indians had given them no authority to do so.

Seattle knew that the haughty little man who had emerged from the ship represented the end of the Indians' dreams and visions as a free people.

So it was with a sense of sadness, mixed with no little contempt and scorn, that Seattle, the friend and benefactor of the white immigrants, rose to speak in response to the new governor.

He chose his words carefully, and, as was the Indian way, he spoke clearly and from the heart. When he had finished, he had uttered one of the most moving eulogies, and prescient admonitions, ever spoken by any man or woman in any language.

His words have been preserved in many documents. Some of these used a later text which was actually a playwright's literary reworking of the speech. The version we reproduce here is the version transcribed by Dr. Henry Smith as he sat on the shores of the Whulge, listening to Seattle speak.

It is as close to the original version as we are likely to get.

▲ ▲ ▲

"We may be brothers after all. We shall see."

— Chief Seattle, 1853

Yonder sky that has wept tears of compassion upon my people for centuries untold, and which to us appears changeless and eternal, may change. Today is fair. Tomorrow it may be overcast with clouds.

My words are like the stars that never change. Whatever Seattle says, the Great Chief at Washington can rely upon with as much certainty as he can upon the return of the sun or the seasons.

The White Chief [Governor Stevens] says that the Big Chief at Washington sends us greetings of friendship and goodwill. This is kind of him, for we know he has little need of our friendship in return.

His people are many. They are like the grass that covers vast prairies.

My people are few. They resemble the scattered trees of a storm-swept plain.

The Great Chief sends us word that he wishes to buy our lands, but is willing to allow us enough to live comfortably. This indeed appears just, even generous, for the red man no longer has rights that he need respect. And the offer may be wise also, as we are no longer in need of an extensive country.

There was a time when our people covered the land as the waves of a wind-ruffled sea cover its shell-paved floor. But that time long since passed away with the greatness of tribes that are now but a mournful memory.

I will not dwell upon, nor mourn over, our untimely decay, nor reproach my white brothers with hastening it, as we too may have been somewhat to blame.

Youth is impulsive. When our young men grow angry at some real or imaginary wrong, and disfigure their faces with black paint, it denotes that their hearts are black, and that they are often cruel and relentless, and our old men and old women are unable to restrain them.

Thus it has ever been. Thus it was when the white man first began to push our forefathers westward.

But let us hope that the hostilities between us may never return. We have everything to lose and nothing to gain.

Revenge by young men is considered gain, even at the cost of their own lives. But old men who stay at home in times of war, and mothers who have sons to lose, know better.

Our good father at Washington — for I presume he is now our father as well as yours, since King George has moved his boundaries further north — our great and good father, I say, sends us word that if we do as he desires, he will protect us. His brave warriors will be to us a bristling wall of strength, and his wonderful ships of war will fill our harbor so that our ancient enemies far to the northward — the Haidas and the Tshimshian — will cease to frighten our women, children, and old men.

Then in reality will he be our father and we his children.

But can that ever be?

Your God is not our God. Your God loves your people and hates mine. He folds His strong protecting arms lovingly about the white man and leads him by the hand as a father leads his infant son. But He has forsaken His red children — if they are really His.

Our God, the Great Spirit, seems also to have forsaken us. Your God makes your people wax strong every day. Soon they will fill all the land. Our people are ebbing away like a rapidly receding tide that will never return.

The white man's God cannot love our people or He would protect them. They seem to be orphans who can look nowhere for help.

How then can we be brothers? How can your God become our God and renew our prosperity and awaken in us dreams of returning greatness?

If we have a common heavenly father He must be partial — or He came to his white children. We never saw him. He gave you laws but had no word for His red children whose teeming multitudes once filled this vast continent as stars fill the firmament.

No, we are two distinct races with separate origins and separate destinies. There is little in common between us.

To us, the ashes of our ancestors are sacred, and their resting place is hallowed ground. You wander far from the graves of your ancestors, and seemingly without regret.

Your religion was written upon tablets of stone by the iron finger of your God so that you could not forget. The red man could never comprehend nor remember it.

Our religion is the traditions of our ancestors — the dreams of our old men, given them in the solemn hours of night by the Great Spirit, and the visions of our sachems — and is written in the hearts of our people.

Your dead cease to love you and the land of their nativity as soon as they pass the portals of the tomb and wander way beyond the stars. They are soon forgotten and never return.

Our dead never forget the beautiful world that gave them being. They still love its verdant valleys, its murmuring rivers, its magnificent mountains, sequestered vales and verdant-lined lakes and bays, and ever yearn in tender, fond affection over the lonely hearted living, and often return from the Great Beyond to visit, guide, console, and comfort them.

Day and night cannot dwell together. The red man has ever fled the approach of the white man, as the morning mist flees before the morning sun.

However, your proposition seems fair and I think that my people will accept it and will retire to the reservation you offer them. Then we will dwell in peace, for the words of the Great White Chief seem to be the words of nature speaking to my people out of dense darkness.

It matters little where we pass the remnant of our days. They will not be many. The Indians' night promises to be dark. Not a single star of hope hovers above his horizon.

Sad-voiced winds moan in the distance. Grim fate seems to be on the red man's trail, and wherever he goes he will hear the approaching footsteps of his fell destroyer and prepare stolidly to meet his doom, as does the wounded doe that hears the approaching footsteps of the hunter.

A few more moons, a few more winters — and not one of the descendants of the mighty hosts that once moved over this broad land or lived in happy homes, protected by the Great Spirit, will remain to mourn over the graves of a people once more powerful and hopeful than yours.

But why should I mourn at the untimely fate of my people? Tribe follows tribe, and nation follows nation, like the waves of the sea. It is the order of nature, and regret is useless.

Your time of decay may be distant, but it surely will come. For even the white man, whose God talked with him as friend with friend, cannot be exempt from the common destiny.

We may be brothers after all. We shall see.

We will ponder your proposition and when we decide, we will let you know. But should we accept it, I here and now make this condition, that we will not be denied the privilege without molestation of visiting at any time the tombs of our ancestors, friends, and children.

Every part of this soil is sacred in the estimation of my people. Every hillside, every valley, every plain and grove, has been hallowed by some sad or happy event in days long vanished.

Even the rocks, which seem to be dumb and dead as they swelter in the sun along the silent shore, thrill with memories of stirring events connected with the lives of my people. And the very dust upon which you now stand responds more lovingly to their footsteps than to yours, because it is rich with the blood of our ancestors and our bare feet are conscious of the sympathetic touch.

Our departed braves, fond mothers, glad, happy-hearted maidens, and even our little children who lived here and rejoiced here for a brief season, will love these somber solitudes, and at eventide they greet shadowy returning spirits.

And when the last red man shall have perished, and the memory of my tribe shall have become a myth among the white men, these shores will swarm with the invisible dead of my tribe.

And when your children's children think themselves alone in the field, the store, the shop, upon the highway, or in the silence of the pathless woods, they will not be alone.

In all the earth there is no place dedicated to solitude. At night, when the streets of your cities and villages are silent, and you think them deserted, they will throng with the returning hosts that once filled them and still love this beautiful land. The white man will never be alone.

Let him be just and deal kindly with my people. For the dead are not powerless.

Dead, did I say? There is no death. Only a change of worlds.

▲ ▲ ▲

About the Editor

Kent Nerburn is editor of two other books in the Classic Wisdom Collection: *Native American Wisdom* and *The Soul of An Indian*. He is also author of the highly acclaimed book, *Letters to My Son — Reflections on Becoming a Man*.

He directed Project Preserve, an award-winning education program in oral history on the Red Lake Ojibwe Reservation, and has been involved in many facets of Indian education. He is a member of the National Indian Education Association and has served as consultant for curriculum development to the American Indian Institute in Norman, Oklahoma.

He holds doctoral degrees in theology and art, and lives with his wife, Louise Mengelkoch, and family in Bemidji, Minnesota.

THE CLASSIC WISDOM COLLECTION
OF
NEW WORLD LIBRARY

AS YOU THINK by James Allen. Edited and with an introduction by Marc Allen.

NATIVE AMERICAN WISDOM. Compiled and with an introduction by Kent Nerburn and Louise Mengelkoch.

THE ART OF TRUE HEALING by Israel Regardie. Edited and updated by Marc Allen.

LETTERS TO A YOUNG POET by Rainer Maria Rilke. Translated by Joan M. Burnham with an introduction by Marc Allen.

THE GREEN THOREAU. Selected and with an introduction by Carol Spenard LaRusso.

POLITICAL TALES AND TRUTH OF MARK TWAIN. Edited and with an introduction by David Hodge and Stacey Freeman.

THE WISDOM OF WOMEN. Selected and with an introduction by Carol Spenard LaRusso.

THE SOUL OF AN INDIAN AND OTHER WRITINGS FROM OHIYESA. Edited and with an introduction by Kent Nerburn.

African American Wisdom. Edited and with an introduction by Reginald McKnight.

The Power of a Woman. Edited and with an introduction by Janet Mills.

The Wisdom of the Great Chiefs. Edited and with an introduction by Kent Nerburn.

New World Library is dedicated to publishing
books and cassettes that help improve
the quality of our lives.

For a catalog of our fine books
and cassettes, contact:

New World Library
58 Paul Drive
San Rafael, CA 94903
Phone: (415) 472-2100
FAX: (415) 472-6131

Or call toll free: (800) 227-3900